LOOK INSIDE

Catherine Chambers

Heinemann Interactive Library
Des Plaines, Illinois

Published by Heinemann Interactive Library,
an imprint of Reed Educational & Professional Publishing,
1350 East Touhy Avenue, Suite 240 West
Des Plaines, IL 60018

Designed by Celia Floyd
Printed in Hong Kong

02 01 00 99 98
10 9 8 7 6 5 4 3 2 1

Library of Congress Cataloging-in-Publication Data
Chambers, Catherine, 1954-
    Sneaker / Catherine Chambers.
      p.   cm. — (Look inside)
    Includes bibliographical references and index.
    Summary: A look at the basic parts of a sneaker and how they are
constructed.
    ISBN 1-57572-624-6
    1. Sneakers—Juvenile literature.   [1. Sneakers. 2. Shoes.]
I. Title II. Series: Chambers. Catherine, 1954-   Look inside.
TS1017.C48 1998
685'.31—dc21

97-31455
CIP
AC

Acknowledgments
The publisher would like to thank the following for permission to reproduce
photographs: Chris Honeywell, pp. 4–21

Cover photograph: Chris Honeywell

Our thanks to Betty Root for her comments in the preparation of this book and
to CICA for their assistance.

Every effort has been made to contact copyright holders of any material reproduced
in this book. Any omissions will be rectified in subsequent printings if notice is given
to the publisher.

Some words are shown in bold, **like this**. You can find
out what they mean by looking in the glossary.

CONTENTS

HERE IS A SNEAKER

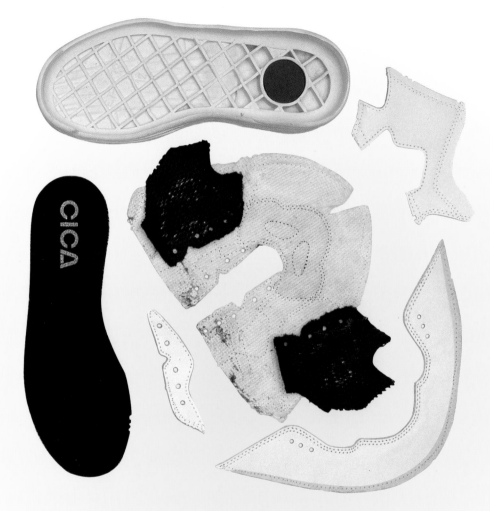

Look at these bits and pieces. Some are large. Others are tiny. Some are soft and spongy. Others are tough and **flexible**, or hard and strong.

Now look at the shapes of the pieces. Most of them are rounded. Some lie flat. They all fit together to make a strong, comfortable sneaker. How is it done?

LONG LACES

Laces are long and thin. They pull the sides of the shoe together so that the shoe stays on your foot. There's some lace leftover to tie a bow. Lace material is loosely **woven**, so it stretches without breaking.

_____ lace

A piece of hard plastic is squeezed around the ends of each lace. This keeps the lace from **fraying**. It also makes the laces easier to slide through the eyelets.

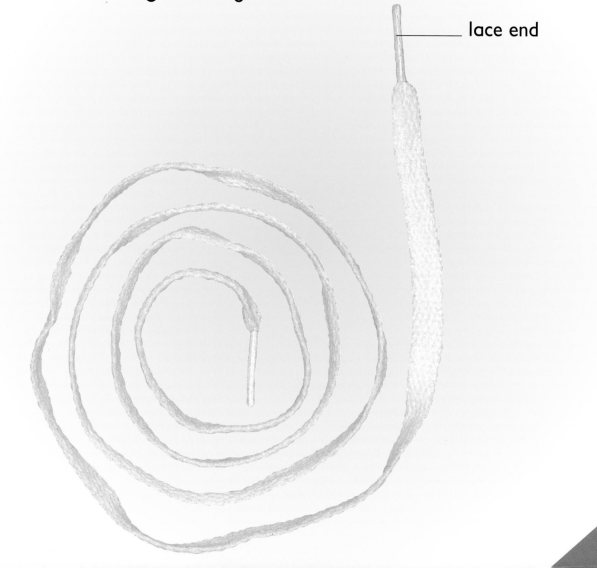

lace end

THE EYELETS

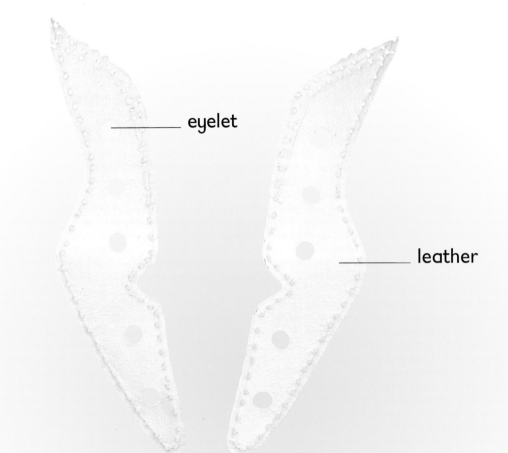

eyelet

leather

Eyelets are holes punched into two pieces of **leather.** The leather is strong and **flexible**. It doesn't tear when the laces are pulled through the eyelets. The leather is also soft, so it doesn't tear the laces.

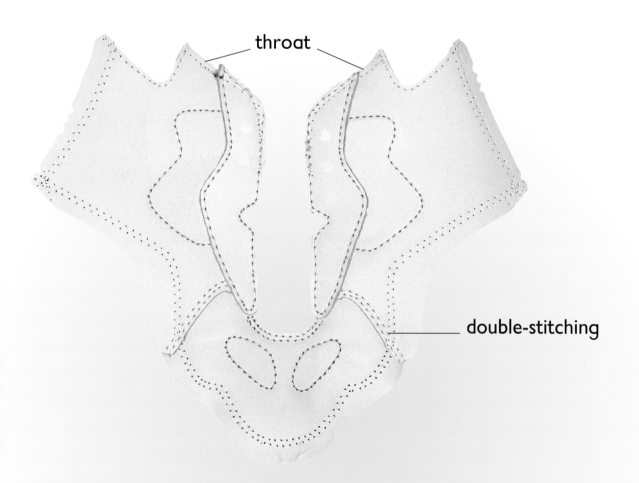

throat

double-stitching

The two pieces of leather are stitched to three others with strong thread. This makes the throat. Two rows of stitches are sewn where extra strength is needed. This is called double-stitching.

HEELS AND TOES

The heel and toe are rounded, like the shape of your foot. And the **leather** is **flexible.** This lets your foot bend. All these pieces help to **support** your foot.

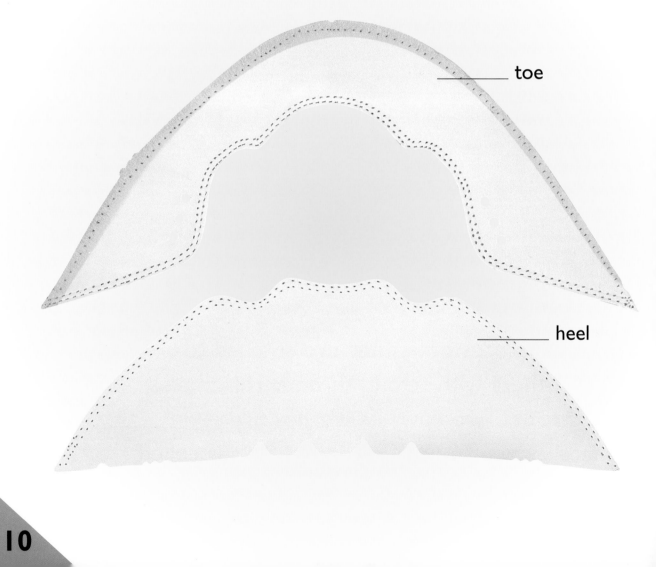

_____ toe

_____ heel

The heel has to be extra strong. It gets a lot of wear. It is stiffened with hard **thermoplastic**. The heel and toe are then stitched to the throat. The whole piece is called the upper.

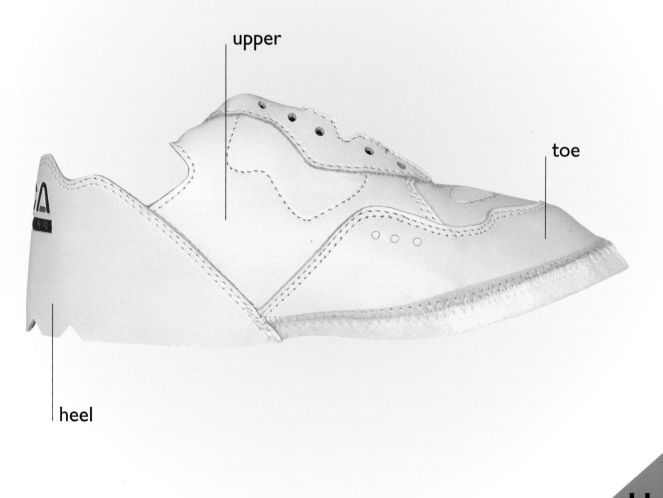

upper

toe

heel

PATTERNS AND COLORS

Leather must be protected. It must also look good. These pieces of leather have a white coating. This can be wiped clean and then polished. Red and black **logos** are pressed into the leather.

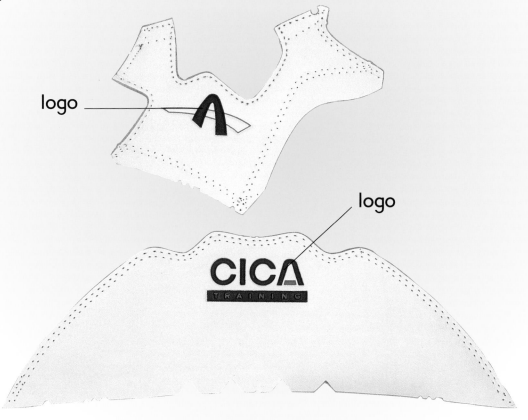

logo

logo

Black and red patterns are made from **woven synthetic** material. They are sewn into holes cut into the leather. These are stitched onto the uppers with the rest of the liners.

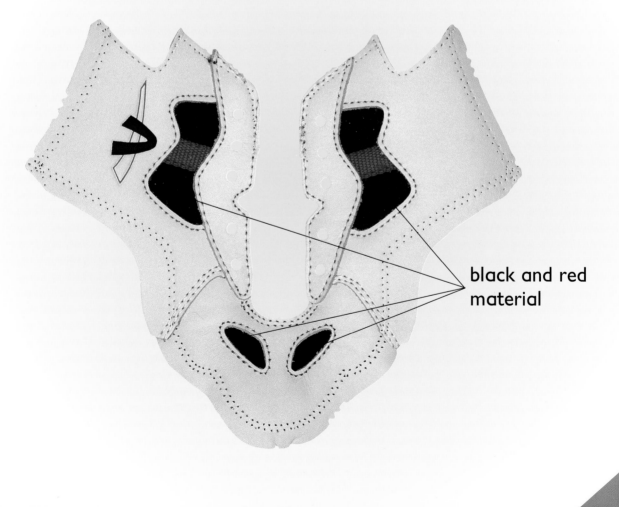

black and red material

THE LINERS

Liners are stitched inside the shoe. Your foot fits right next to the liners. Liners are made from **synthetic** material. They are thin and soft. They are also strong.

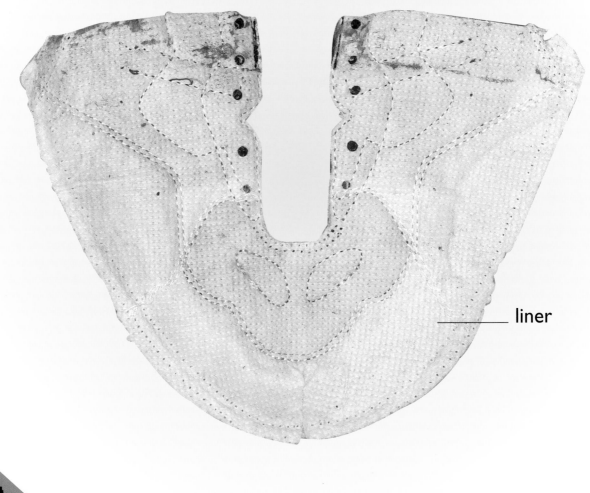

_____ liner

Soft fabric and spongy filler are used on the tongue and around the heel. This keeps them from rubbing against your foot. A label with a **logo** is stitched to the tongue. Now they are ready for the soles.

heel pad

filler

CICA
TRAINING

tongue

STRONG SOLES

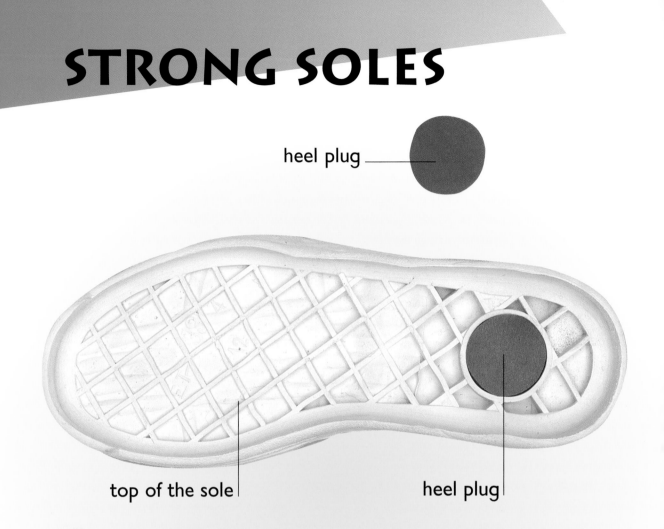

heel plug

top of the sole

heel plug

Soles are made from **polyurethane**. This makes them thick and springy. It also makes them tough but **flexible**. The blue heel plug disk is made of polyurethane foam. It protects your heels when you run and jump.

The top of the sole is flat. This is where your foot rests. The bottom of the sole is **grooved**. This helps the sole to grip the ground. The soles are glued onto the uppers with a cement. A powerful **pressure process** is used.

grooves

underneath the sole

INSOLES

Insoles are put on top of the sole, where your foot rests. They are made from pieces of **leather.** These are the pieces left over from making the uppers. The leather is made into a **pulp**. It is then pressed, dried, and cut into the shape of a foot.

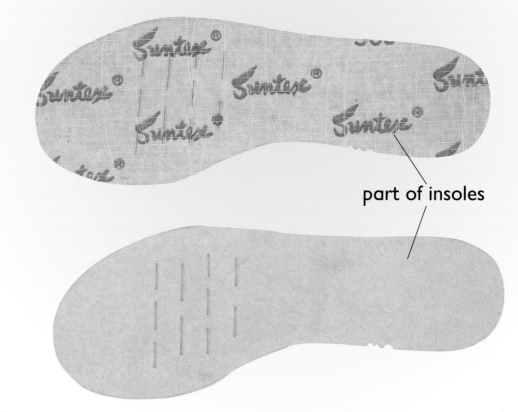

part of insoles

The sneaker is still hard inside. It needs soft, springy insoles. These are made from **polyurethane** foam. A tough, stretchy material is stuck on top.

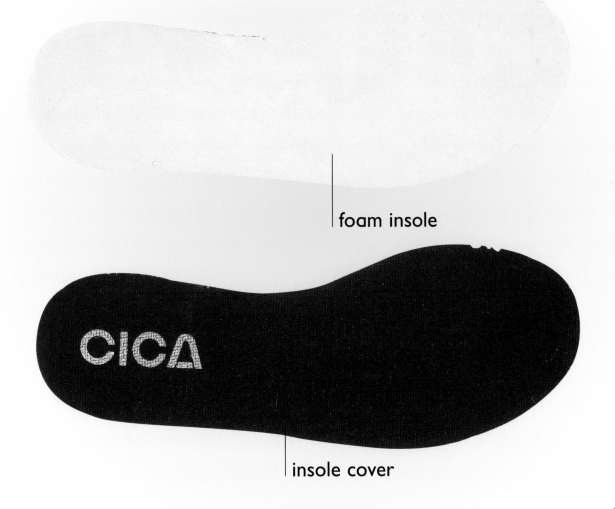

foam insole

insole cover

LET'S WALK!

Here are the sneakers. All the bits and pieces have been put together. There are other kinds of sneakers, too. Some have plastic bubbles in the soles. Some have flashing lights. Some sneakers even glow in the dark. Others pump up if you press the tongue!

Sneakers are tough, springy, and fun. You can run in them. You can play in them. They're good for your feet, too.

GLOSSARY

flexible   bends easily

fraying   when a material wears away

grooved   cut with deep lines

leather   material made from animal skins, used for many purposes

logos   symbols that show who made something

polyurethane   a type of plastic

pressure process   stuck together with great force by machine

pulp   mashed up material mixed with a liquid

support   to hold firmly

synthetic   made by people, not natural

thermoplastic   very hard manmade material

woven   when threads are crossed over each other to make a material

MORE BOOKS TO READ

Barnes, Lilly. *Lace Them Up*. New York: Hyperion, 1992.

Mason, Kate. *The Shoe Book: Learn to Tie Your Shoes!* Mahwah, NJ: Troll Communications, 1996.

Spiers, John. *Shoes, Shoes, Shoes*. Racine, Wis: Western Publishing Company, 1995.

Strauss, Lucy. *The Story of Shoes*. Austin, Tex: Raintree Steck-Vaughn, 1989.

Young, Robert. *Sneakers: The Shoes We Choose*. Morristown, NJ: Silver Burdett Press, 1991.

INDEX